Portraits

Portraits

POEMS
B. Z. Niditch

Series Volume I
Alternating Current Press
Boulder, Colorado

Portraits
B. Z. Niditch
©2019 Alternating Current Press

All material in *Portraits* is the property of its respective creator and may not be used or reprinted in any manner without express permission from the author or publisher, except for the quotation of short passages used inside of an article, criticism, or review. Printed in the United States of America. All rights reserved. All material in *Portraits* is printed with permission.

Alternating Current
Boulder, Colorado
alternatingcurrentarts.com

ISBN-10: 1-946580-09-0
ISBN-13: 978-1-946580-09-2
First Edition: February 2019

Table of Contents

Beckett's Morning ·11
Braque ·12
Before Liberation ·13
Albert Einstein ·14
Alexander Archipenko ·15
Jerusalem Day ·16
1929 ·17
August Days ·18
T. E. Lawrence ·19
Soirée ·20
Alfred Jarry ·21
Poulenc Cello Sonata ·22
César Vallejo's Night ·23
Else's Time ·24
Shreveport ·25
Thom Gunn's Shower ·26
Rauschenberg: Sugar Night ·27
Mr. Facing ·28
Philippe Denis ·29
Meeting Robert Lowell ·30
Music School ·31
Hearing Busoni ·32
The Last ·33
Out of Exile ·34
Chelsea Hotel: 1968 ·35
Maria Callas ·36
Neruda's Day ·37
Bukowski ·38
Reverdy ·39
Joan Miró ·40
Remember Rimbaud ·41
Burma ·42
Hockney at the West Coast ·43
At Bruckner's "Mass" ·44
To Allen Tate ·45
Dylan Thomas' Night ·46
Apollinaire ·47
A Day with Kerouac ·48
Breton ·49
Luis Buñuel's *Viridiana* ·50
Bob Dylan ·51
René Char ·52
Missing Person ·53
Lautréamont by the Seine ·54
Chagall's Century ·55
Desnos ·56
Motherwell's "The Voyage" ·57
Milhaud ·58
A Political Man: 1966 ·59
Valéry ·60
Max Jacob ·61
Acting Up ·62
Leni R. at 100 ·63
Artaud ·64
Canetti's Ground ·65
Simone Weil ·66
Stalin Is Dead ·67
A Man Named Walt ·68
Shostakovich ·69
Central Park ·70
Saint-John Perse ·71
Walden Pond ·72
Yves Bonnefoy ·73
1968 ·74
Much of the Night ·76
Alain Bosquet ·77
Hampton Beach ·78
Akhmatova ·79
Paul Goodman's Night ·80
Ra'hel's Time ·82
1940 ·83
Rilke ·84
Franz Marc ·85
Rubén Darío's Voyage ·86
Francis Ponge ·87
Retrospective ·88
Marilyn ·89
O. V. de L. Milosz ·90

Umberto Saba ·91
Keats ·92
Celan in 1950 ·93
Frank O'Hara in SoHo ·94
Cendrars ·95
Albert Marquet's Posters ·96
Jacques Roubaud ·97
Kokoschka ·98
Marina Tsvetaeva ·99
Jam Session ·100
A Century Past ·101
Queneau ·102
Looking Away ·103
December Days ·104
Mondrian ·105
Cioran's Wager ·106
Aragon ·107
Edmond Jabès ·108
"Out in the Open" ·109
At the Savoy ·110
Brecht ·111
Flame ·112
The Wharf ·113
Larbaud ·114
Romantics ·115
Ned Rorem ·116
Mishima ·117
Rimbaud ·118
Jacques Prévert ·119
Klee ·120
Marcel Proust ·121
Visiting Helen Vendler ·122
Bei Dao ·123
Lorca at Seville ·124
Edward Albee ·125
Alain Veinstein ·126
On Beacon Hill ·127
André Derain ·128
Kierkegaard ·129
Brâncuși ·130
Jaccottet ·131

James Joyce ·132
Kurosawa ·133
Baudelaire's Lament ·134
Stefan George ·135
Jun Takami ·136
Debussy Sonata ·137
Borges' Last Day ·138
John Wieners ·139
Jules Supervielle ·140
Urban Reading ·141
Klee's Angel ·142
Soupault ·143
Proust and Vermeer ·144
Tell Me ·145
Jean Follain ·146
Kafkaesque Images ·147
Manhattan Riffs ·148
Hocquard ·149
A Letter to James Merrill ·150
On Cambridge Common ·151
Dalí's "Enigma" ·152
Weil ·153
Joy Street ·154
Picasso's "Corrida" ·155
Paul Claudel ·156
The Print ·157
A New World ·158
Camille Claudel ·159
Going Underground ·160
Soutine's Painting ·162
Hugo Claus ·163
Recognition ·164
Louis Aragon ·165
All These Earthly Things ·166
Summer Blues ·168
Warhol's Factory ·169
Pierre Jean Jouve ·170
Sartre's Tongue ·171
Tanguy's "Dark Garden" ·172
James Schuyler ·173

The Wardenclyffe Series is a collection of books preserving the words of Beat and Post-Beat poets whose work first saw publication prior to the new millennium and the digital age. Alternating Current Press eagerly acquires the work of voices past to influence the voices of the future.

Introduction from the Editor

I'm a leftover remnant from the cut-n-paste zine days, first commercially publishing as a pre-teen in 1993, and selling thousands of newsprint zines and photocopied chapbooks to readers in over 50 countries by the age of 14. Most of us gave it up and became adults; I kept going—archiving, cataloging, and publishing the Post-Beats and the era of writers that bridged that gap between Kerouac and Internet. Many of those authors are gone now, swallowed by the advent of Submittable, blogs, electronic communication, and the vanity-publishing deluge; or simply *gone* gone, defeated in our endless battle against *time*. Those writers trusted us pre-digital small-pressers with their words, and it is important to me that I keep those words alive as we introduce them to a whole new generation.

    B. Z. Niditch was born in 1943, a war-child coming of age in the era of Beat and Post-Beat poets. He first sent us his work in the mid-1990s, and we published his pieces in some of our earliest poetry anthologies in 1995 and '96, and then regularly after that, including two chapbooks, until the mid-2010s, when correspondence slowed. I best classify his work as just-Post-Beat, with the stream-of-consciousness flow that demarcates Beat and his love of jazz, but with a heavy political influence from war-time French poets and a nature influence that comes from life on the New England coast, met with the immediacy of traditional haiku. In his own words, he calls himself a "political poet," though his work is varied and touches often on seasons, music, theater, nature, pop culture, artwork, films, and analyses of the works of The Greats. This collection features brief homages, profiles, and "portraits" of those who've influenced Niditch's work or thoughts, compiled over decades of shifting cultures and tastes. Take a step inside his frame.

Leah Angstman

Portraits

Beckett's Morning

Absence of concern
moves two characters' surprise
in expectant geography
but the pronouns add up
to the language of rain,
two passports
here in Paris.
No one claims the colossi
of the nimbus,
no one knows the numbers
on the intersection.
Somewhere near the Métro
the actors are assembling
in early canopy,
windows of the amphitheater
are bare but collapsing
reducing interrogation
of crystalline speech
in abandoned avenues
melancholy landscapes
in the subtle backdrop
of final moments
in murmured voice
of a detached century.

Braque

It must hurt
for the first hour,
the palette alone
in a tiny doorway
where light betrays
even the easiest sun
at the boat on the beach.
When browsing the horizon
a wish hangs on,
the hand must have pain.

Before Liberation

Can you hear us
still calling out
your initials
from the highest walls
at the Last Supper
of blood oranges.
Here dark roses
cannot live
near the agonized notes
of Mahler's children
and the unkempt score
of Wajda's *Ashes and Diamonds*.

Sleep on your bed unmade,
hear whispers of straw
by draped full dress
of brown-shirted thugs
fresh from war's weariness
in willing animal skins
of masked galley slaves,
by overcoats of clerks
in green rooms
who tally death notices,
annihilating loss of sky.

Albert Einstein

Suitcase. Suitcase.
"Surely this one
is not for me."
Numbers to resolve
not on human arms.

Roses in thorn bushes
on student yard gates
of Viennese spring
left forever
unspeakable
in the human sunlight.

Alexander Archipenko

Why is it dark
down the perennials
of unsliced paint
on a visitor's day
tangling praise out
of wrapped ruined heroes
and rusty weeping
on snowy sofas?
No bare side
is ever taken back.

Jerusalem Day

Schubert
by a jar of roses
somewhere in the old city.

Dawn is constant,
an alcove of spring
Jerusalem returns early

always composed,
blushing,
a rarefied cadenza.

You put on new earrings
from the Dead Sea.

1929

for Walter Benjamin

In the morning,
an instant half of bread
murdered day-old cake
taken along
Berlin's darkness.
Today the currency
in *Trauerspiel*
is in pantomime,
everything is disdain,
boredom cries incognito
yet somehow cosmopolitan
feels the folding
of historical hate.
Slogans from scrawny hands
outnumber surplus human value.
Fed up with weariness
I sidle into a tailor shop,
I ask to be clothed
in this untenanted earth.

August Days

for Donald Justice, 1925–2004

August days roll like dust
luminous as the sea,
a faraway oriole
lingers to play in the wind,
circling skies turn about
from clouds
hiding hurricane forecasts
along hightide beaches.

You will do everything
to outlast summer's caress,
make vows at the lighthouse
not to listen to weary tourists
boarding school buses
for one final trek to the ocean,
or waking three children
falling over their camp gear
who find a junkyard cat
near a daylong newlywed retreat.

With lightning interference
form the radio reception
full of war
and runaway rumors,
you return to the pitiless shore
where death
like a requiem for Pegasus
plays its final horseshoe.

T. E. Lawrence

Only the desert
remembers daybreak.
In a landlocked memory
swords confound
the mountain's peace.

Soirée

Off Tremont Street
in Jamesian fashion
you hid Remy de Gourmont
in the yellow book
over the veiled portico.
As twin Cremonas
played Bach's
"Double Concerto,"
gents and ladies
eyed Boston
on the card table.
Mrs. Gardner shone
with the Berenson boy
passionate for Uccello, Vermeer,
a Venetian ring,
hands in her newest sable
and parodying Edward Lear.

You carried a bundle
of expatriate letters,
wine by your elbow
of cold connoisseurs
enjoying Japanese china
along the bric-a-brac wall,
admiring the past Whistler
and scripts of Wilde,
you remember the soirées
and last November's teas
where you read *Childe Harold*
in Byronic company.
Now it's another fall to Rome
by way of Greece and then home.

Alfred Jarry

Caught red-nosed
slicked back into bed,
Parisian cafés open early
offering any erased lips,
legs were cold cream
drawing-back words
tint the windowpanes
screw the party lines
the slender disguises
behind pink eyelids.
Life is proximity
reared near the bust,
the masked woman
with the cartridge belts.

Your mouth is a belly
the titmouse of a big city.
Freud is only a stalactite
carrying to sweep away,
Marx plucks a great reptile
recalling your last *déjà vu*,
a blindfolded politician
mechanical starfish
vertigo in a sad pantomime,
a pleading look back
refusing Vichy carrots,
any meal with crownshirt cadres
the foreign bodies offering
death on Salome platters.

Poulenc Cello Sonata

A landslide of notes
detaches all colors,
rising mirrors
split open atonality
phrases ephemeral
as wildflowers.

César Vallejo's Night

Night travels the field
among a hundred days.
Your bed enters darkness
on a bridge of departure
from poor man
working dreams
against tomorrow.
The heated sky opens
beneath an indifferent sun,
unlocking a map of clouds
from Peruvian cosmogony.

Your nightmares enlighten
the shadows of corpses
along vast mountainsides.
No doubt, the earth
photographs your long face
among the pine leaves
trampling over your grave,
petals fall on meadows
pressed by your doorway
granting hours of eternity
from those who won't forget.

Else's Time

for Else Lasker-Schüler, in memoriam

Else,
you were raised
with us,
written off
in exiled letters
as a child's seer
in the language of nature,
deciphered in the scripts
from the ages and stars,
painting our eternities
in shadows of grief,
escaping every scent
that the earth buries
between millennia,
yet the skies drip blood
from sisters and brothers
who mourn our nights,
transfuse our deaths,
recreating the ineffable.

Shreveport

On indigo sea
lost for six hours
looking for dawn
in the ready rain
gulls on the beach
life from fog
paintings like Cézanne
wrap my arms
full of oranges.

Thom Gunn's Shower

In the laundry room
tongues whisper
from resident holes
washing out
dry runs of the night
amid a sad Achilles.

Hands ring out
tropical tableau
from hot blankets
trapped Trojans
rinsed time
to neck
in a sorry labyrinth.

A guy up from Bath
pants from his sleeves,
Thom handily scalds
and warmly presses
a lost Ulysses
without an address.

Rauschenberg: Sugar Night

In the cataracts
of "Sugar Night"
you expect
the city to be moved
to sleep in the instant
of asking electricity.

Let's go
past reverberating mirrors
lines of scorned tongues
where the moon
has a reprobate quarter
and balconies
slide from Friday on Saturday.

Beside you
this night is imperceptible
when grief is transparent
and bread is pillaged
for a four-seasoned refugee
and white
is blacker than mineral springs
outside the chloroform street pulse.

Mr. Facing

You met him
near the Southern-crossed fence.
He lifted weights, he said,
you were frozen from the snow
a runaway by the river and Dung Gate
where men like him
follow the vague light
and travel the neon jungle
carrying his sailor eyes
without an ID
and you were hungry
from the taunted night,
and in the gray trellis
of the half moon
you made what makes him tick.
You want to put on
his motorcycle jacket
and he says he will love you
in the morning.
All you remember
is his breath,
the tobacco-colored hair
you found in your mouth.

Philippe Denis

On the daily carpet
words follow the leaves,
a dog in a narrow alley
rests under chestnut trees.

Meeting Robert Lowell

Into your creaking office
with ivy-toned wisdom,
I'm carrying Catullus
but fearing thirst and hell.
You were defenseless
in a wizened gray sweater,
crazy and cold
muttering about
the withered evergreen
the nutjob Hitler
sullen Berryman
and an ambulance
to McLean Hospital
on the way.

Outside your window
snowflakes quivered,
you recited in Japanese
asking for Tate and sake,
and I'm trembling
to share a few stanzas
from my creased notebook
and wounded sensibility.
A circle of affection
yields a shadow
across the room.

Music School

Bach plays in sunlight,
each note lives out
its tiny dawn,
in another corner
a young Pavlova
floats by
as first swan
to water,
the winds overhear
students of arias
letting illusions
of fevered love,
in soundproof space
dust flies off
the cadenza's page
of a century's regrets,
now a tough glance
at the back muscles
of junior Nijinsky.
At the bar,
it's breaking time
for the clarinet soloist's
diminished chord
in a doorway of riffs.

Hearing Busoni

The early fever
passes by your tongue,
legendary keys whisper
in sleepless sonata,
"piano, piano."

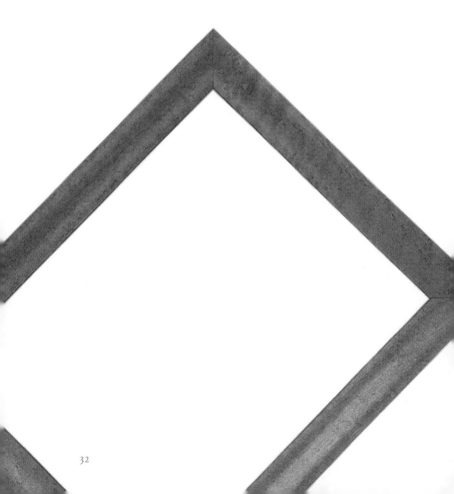

The Last

The last history exam
held by your small fingers,
Simone,
in windowless schoolroom
receiving highest marks,
casting yourself
in the last seat,
fasting with the Last Supper
through every distress,
the world's image
untangled for the deeply etched.

Out of Exile

for Richard Murphy

To tell with ease
about Ash Wednesday
counting ship windows
when apologies of exiles
never will work out
on the open vessels
leaking out of centuries
on floorboards
full of cabin fevers.

It's never too late
from cloth, parchment, and hair
to know when you will return.
You lean against St. Bridget's
mitigated for penance
trying to picture Leopold Bloom
kiss his door's mezuzah.

A nightmare
mocks up blood
to scrub a martyr's deck
in remorseful sleep,
of every grinning blame
posterity is a lost tomb.
You cannot kick or whistle
against the cedar gates.

Chelsea Hotel: 1968

At dinner
eating escargot
and poached salmon
with a household goddess
once known as Rick,
you still complain
about pop culture,
Candy Darling,
once your basic ex-Jesuit
fearing junkies,
pornography,
and Mother Teresa,
you're now
a fearsome transvestite
living with strung-out
drag queens
housed in the Chelsea.

Maria Callas

Periscopes of the Aegean
opening night,
your body of memory
notes in a sunglass,
the same great Medea.

Neruda's Day

With your splintered voice
charred from sandpits
by flowerless fields,
on a walking stick
you survey a sleeping sun
somewhere in Valparaíso.
Shaken by a posture of wind
the day revives you
with single-light glance
at the general injustice
of a hungry earth time.

A child rises under a bridge
shouting a manna of words
wishing for a taste of bread
from a brushfire of solidarity.
You pass by honeyed trees
your giant footprints
on a Rust Belt road
wanting to be boundless
as a sea of feathered eagles
covers tattooed sky.

Bukowski

Wild wordsmith
in your great spaces
of L.A. horror's beauty
will always come back
in a drinking mug
of a mirror's well
effacing barracks of chaos
along peppered railyards
in phosphorescent darkness
tearing your daybreak flesh
pretending death
is a fire next door
to a cold flat
cherry-picking your lovers
in a narcissistic bathtub
filled with vodka.
No one is there
to patch up
your bloody bandages
from the last
tar-bar fight
panting from
your exhaustive pain
in fatigues old as poetry.

Reverdy

A stone
face winds
the name
we cannot utter.

Joan Miró

In the passer-by letters
the fixed sky
fought for memories
in the endless glance
across cinnamon clouds
from anarchic ascent
flutters bird and cassia
in knotted storm.

In a failing laughter
not looking down
to the gamut of green
from observed eyes
brags a renunciation.
Crumbled morning
blind-arrows angels
in its fated kingdom.

Remember Rimbaud

I'm more than a stranger
from Paris on leave,
a deserter
from every dune
absorbed by the sea
exiled from two continents
absent from all schools
not eaten by beefcake
reaching for solitaire
mortgaged to the night
annulled by any bonds
escaped from nine Commandments
evading all occupations
without shoes or goodbyes
disregarding chitchat
at every subway stop,
in fact, unpierced
by my guiltless right ear.

Burma

for Aung San Suu Kyi

Blue scarf
trembles
over windy hills.
Signs are memories
of injustices,
landlocked daylight,
flowers by doorways.
A mouth is screened,
letters voiceless,
closed handkerchiefs,
a fresh bandage
in waiting sunrise.

Hockney at the West Coast

Dipping your toes
and fingers by canvas
in dawn's torso,
shedding caresses
of windjammer waves.

At Bruckner's "Mass"

An unwashed Viennese
sneaks into the concert hall
listening to Bruckner's "Mass"
without paying admission.

He's one of the masses
himself
though he yearns to be
a grand conductor.

Splashes of lager
stain a stolen overcoat,
he claims to be an artist.

Others think of him
as a house painter
but he'll have his last laugh,
this watercolorist, Adolf.

To Allen Tate

Confederate of words
now departed into themes
of more than one believes
by never-forgotten fields
as though one's ode
sung upward
when there is something unseen
a river sound dreaming
looking down a cavern
cotton combs thrown to the wind
through insatiate crystal ears
grace which captures
holly leaves
of every fall.

Dylan Thomas' Night

Wind riddled nightfall
by two drowsy glasses,
you devour hyperbole
from molehils of sleep
restless on unmade bed
full of swaggering pain
and thrashed-out complaints
near a moldy basket
stuffed with a week's worth
of unfinished plays,
you sidle into empty sheets
red-eyed and buttonless
between cadences and blackouts
in your disillusioned twentieth
embracing mixers of words
from shadowy lexicon
drunk with solitude.

Apollinaire

Raising the void
an apostle's footsteps
you skin a moonless memory
crossdressing
the first apple eaten.

A Day with Kerouac

Making the rounds
in a fever of rain
high even
at daylight,
Jack, hear me out,
you're still being stalked
by a dusk-to-dawn fan
who won't leave
admitting rooms
of the underworld.
Though solitary
you're really a rogue pirate
hiding out
near Provincetown
with fish stories
and double secrets.

Yet in spite of allegories
in your skeptical head
you drink absinthe
from a Cape Cod mug
embroidered with wildflowers
murdering French bread
and blood oranges,
your nerves twist
at the tar-bar piano.
A pint-sized hunger squeezes
your stale mouth
of bottomed-out elixir,
you take a hunter's revolver
shooting out poetry.

Breton

Caressing night arms
with yellow umbrellas
by beach trees,
dreams half speak.

Luis Buñuel's Viridiana

Unknown semblance
of unconscious misfits
ex-camera voices
in a disillusioned posed hour
surreal in massive space
and wingbeats of horror
when the sixth cold sweat
memorizes time,
your eyelids overtired
in an evaporated cast
a few scenes apart,
on empty couch,
a delirium of questions
marks your breathing
of theatrical dressing.

Bob Dylan

I heard you
with perpetual motion
in a hotel room
you rehearsed in
somewhere.
The Manhattan elixir
seemed invisible
on your teething mouth
full of painted poems
in electric July
without a draught of air,
your guitar, half deep
in rhymes
through the soundproof room,
riffs grow younger
from solitary cold sweats
near the lemon-hearted piano.
You carry on
trying to make time
in your one-fingered rant.

René Char

Eternity cannot exit
an apple sky
or orange foliage
peeling a black raindrop day.

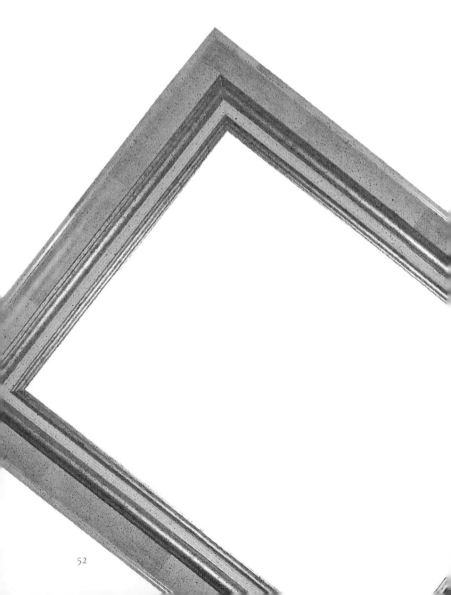

Missing Person

Sunlight
keeps its distance.
I'm silently staring
at an open window
under azure sky
for any moonstone sign
to face drowsy clouds
for angels of death.

With sleepwalking
madness,
daily nightmares cut off
infantilized cries
of every motioning memory.
In my own hoarseness,
irony has ceased
to bathe any patience,
closing hours
of my own shutters.

Lautréamont by the Seine

Gliding your window
the sea is a gossamer,
you lose your weariness
to surf a gothic eye
in mirror-well waves.

Waking choked
with inkwell cosmic stares,
landscapes ricocheted
in harried winds,
you risk premonitions
recounting each albatross.

Chagall's Century

Ensuring in sound
praising sepulture
from ash and slight
dazzling correspondents
of solitude
in elixirs of blood
from a century
of white darkness.

Desnos

Your limbs hurt
by the dogs' howl.
No time to sound
with raids of death
in the wide ravine.

Motherwell's "The Voyage"

The idea is the ocean
in a loss of three oranges
from an elective nature
of blood, drunken boats, reverie
in graffiti roses
ruling the streets
only timeless whispers remain
captains of hostility,
Billy Budd dreams,
children shivering from rain,
boycotts of passengers
with tickets to nowhere.

Milhaud

Clouds, rivulets
in Provence,
bee's eye Pierrian roses,
sunshine opens
augmented piano notes
along the shade of river.

A Political Man: 1966

I hear
Kirill Kondrashin
is conducting *Swan Lake*
but who is the red flame
next to you
whose dad went to Spain
to fascist fight
and came home
crippled in silence
but writes memoirs
made from Havana cigar smoke
with his new arms and legs
with rage
at the strength
that left the body
the city's dusty disappointments
that turns into Picasso
sheets of "Guernica" paints.
It's said
that the police
are still after him
for his politics.
With his new Russian
newspaper clippings
downstairs
he is pacing like Pablo, the cat.

Valéry

No explanations for sunlight
au revoir for pale words,
we still tremble
from history's void
yet Thursday's rain showers
the passionate remorse
of unsigned letters,
offers valid fervor of memoirs
colors, sound
questions the countenance of clouds.
An empty signature
intersects a page
of the impalpable.

Max Jacob

Magnifying glasses
carrying on
historical bins,
trains on time zero
baggage crosses
fourteen stations.

Acting Up

You are watching Woody
and being shamed
to laughter's twinkle
having returned home late
from acting rehearsal,
you have no hatred
for the understudy,
you write on the wall
of the kitchenette.

Your honeyed larynx
has been cough-dropped
after five hours' exhaustion
and you appear faceless,
calmly ask forgiveness,
until two tiny wine glasses
are broken in the fireplace
with no real answer
for high-summer bitterness
except when you are mute
and all engaged voices
are on remote.

Leni R. at 100

What staying power
that all your Gypsies
suddenly, without a cue
disappear like extras
for a movie.

Isn't it funny
you knew nothing
about politics
yet you have a meeting
with Adolf at four

on your calendar
and watch,
millions will march
to the same tune
and camera.

While others suddenly
and mysteriously
disappear,
you live on.

A mystery, life.

Artaud

Nights in negation
of an assassin's art,
bivouac nature
acting out drama's lines.

Canetti's Ground

Every horizon
resembles wormwood
Hiroshima at daybreak
"Guernica" in late afternoon.
Early thunder
huddles us like children
in hail of Caesars,
but you, Elias,
cannot even dust off
your overcoat.
Instead you take on
twenty lashes
for every centurion,
you watch camp guards
pass out favors
like party invites,
as the smart-dressed torturers
hide away from the crowd,
letting the angel of light
invisibly encircle
a blood-red carpet
of snow.

Simone Weil

Simone,
from your undiscovered bed
to the rainy north
all sky is blue-hearted
by your elbow's blue door.
A ragged solitude guides you
out of the dusky book
to a child's deadened hunger
by red lava fields,
at your right window
apocalyptic streets of roses
butterflies echo
by bullfights and icons,
you pull your covers
of crisscross feathers
over stubborn earth.

Stalin Is Dead

The four-toed toad
drawing a yellow wolf
on pitiless papers
has an unfriendly visitor.

Death's one-eyed scissor
who trampled his enemies
is himself worn out
on Haman's night.

A Man Named Walt

The very man named Walt
with one marble blue eye
and navy cap
rests in the fields
under morning sun.
It was rumored
he was once in opera
before the war
had taken away
his voice.

Transfixed
like a weightlifter
or a foreign god
when he put me on
his tattooed shoulders
filled with mermaids and roses,
he turns bluer than birds
drinking from a wine cup,
with an air about him
he drew my picture
in black ink.

Everyone in town
is afraid of him.
They say he was kidnapped
at my age
by Martians or Gypsies
and could make war or love
with birds, flowers, and runaways
for the asking.
He sleeps on a straw blanket,
there is a book of poems
illustrated, near him.

Shostakovich

A cello left
in a row of cellars,
a cantor's voice
from the marsh.

Central Park

Overhearing a quarrel
part French, part Italian,
"You must decide now
like musical notes
if you will act up
with B-sharp or harmony
to complain or be compliant,"
as the couple efface
every empty gesture
for an operatic evening
going into a frenzy
of Maria Callas or Caruso
accusations,
offing each other
throwing opera tickets
and glasses
near the park bench
and a voiceless poet
with several unwritten notebooks
announces to his own alter ego,
"Let's go to *Tosca*."

Saint-John Perse

The heron and starfish
every wakened gull
listen to the strange sky
opening a floodlit path
upward on banal clouds.

You passed it all
in sullen gray abyss
nadirs of foliage
a spring, your refuge
lucid fountains,
fevered waters,
undulant celebration.

Walden Pond

Propped up with Thoreau
and benevolent Hawthorne
embracing evergreens
under hereditary skies,
cicadas cloud
the frenzied crickets
with ruddy winds,
a butterfly on your shadow
shines low at noonday
indifferent to half light,
blinking rays scatter over
pebbles on the pond.

Yves Bonnefoy

Trembling chimeras
from skeptical inkwells
draw along the shore,
paint the undivided sea.

1968

hideous napalm
over rain-swept diary,
a photographic shower
somewhere in the tapered light,
a deserter in denim
near an L.A. topless bar,
a defunct clock
moves a flashback camera,
a daily nightmare kicks
in reds, greens, and yellows
off the rooming-house sheet,
a West novel falls
from the locust ceiling,
Jane Russell emerges
from *The Outlaw*
at two in the morning,
Hitchcock's *The Birds*
scream and an evangelist
repents on the broken television
smashing the money-changed
laundered bills,
giving away his gay son
who runs to escape
the managed whiz kid
band of warfare,
the waitress from Las Vegas
here for a convention
of the Third Order of Mary
orders a double Bloody Mary
from the bartender
whose husband became a woman
because life had to change
and Dick disinfects Southeast Asia
and deodorizes Communism

after the Hollywood Ten,
in California he eats grapes
and the pregnant black woman
at the campaign stop says
"Nixon's the One"
and a transvestite carries
a sign to "Bring the Boys Home,"
the boys do not come home
as nuclear fallout
enveloping Nevada
drifts over the nation's
supermarket to the world.

Much of the Night

for Dahlia Ravikovitch, 1936–2005

To Gehenna with death
every thorn lives with you
in an endless flood.
Your blueprints wash
the sand and arid earth
in the harried holy city
with a few stones nearby.
Everywhere blood speaks
through much of the night
open for the sea, poor sister
astonishing the eucalyptus,
the sun nourishes the rocks
feeding on five thousand pages,
half-old history, new geography.
Doves from perches
line ancient fortresses
of the desert carcass
speaking to your heart,
evicted by the earth.

Alain Bosquet

The search in fire
of the lost
inexplicable stars and stones
of the second ashen war.

Hampton Beach

With new 9 a.m. binoculars
you survey the cliff dwellers
huge beef embracing
bruised motorcycles
heated leather and tattoos
near the turnpike
where two nymphs dance
to James Brown
in the tumbleweed
giggling with eagerness
will pass a half hour
with perfumed surf
stinging their nostrils
waves curled
in a panic attack
and big-eyed Joe
the eternal lifeguard
knowing he's being watched
removes his Roman shirt
and flips through a roadmap
for the shy tourists
who deposit towels,
lotion, and laughter
in Apollo's path.

Akhmatova

Waiting for her son's eyes
on the coldest Monday,
black-blue lights
over a tiny bird's dawn.

Paul Goodman's Night

And Paul Goodman
you found that guy
at the bus stop,
20 but really younger
in your eyes and even his own
with the pale white skin.
He was a runaway from life
in a different way
from yours
and he was youth,
your lost one,
the one you and he
would never find again
and you know
if you don't talk
or open up
or open him up
or pick a fight
you will lose the night.

The night
you kissed every part
of him and your life
away, you wanted his secret.
He wouldn't give it away,
was it money he was after
or drugs or Daddy or you,
a sociologist of love
just like the lost
thrown out of
yet beautiful to you
used, abused even by you
for love, for hurt, for justice
but who can guess or care

for the one
with the pale skin
and the shorts and sneakers.
He knew he had something
you wanted,
a whole lot of things,
youth, platonic beauty,
innocence, a mask
of guilt of his own failings
and in the night
of the pale skin
when everything came off
you could sing
you, too, could sing
you were happy
you were not alone
even if the world
condemned you.

Ra'hel's Time

Out of Russian exile
childhood takes root
by the sea,
a star around your neck.
You, between lake and desert,
spy a dove's wing
so high
on the newborn land,
a universe appears
in your soft palm.

1940

1. Consciousness (out of being

2. the jazz blue shirts

3. in Russian blouses)

4. in a mean Munch

5. covering fascism

6. hiding a Gorky miniature

7. falling longer victims

8. without a sleep house

9. blood is policy

10. out of arrangements.

Rilke

Kept in sunlight
until an hour's ruin,
an angel never dozes
by winds alone.

Franz Marc

Because up here
the legends are fragrant,
ruminating,
an eye has waved
the subpoena of emigrants
in the air cries
recognizing spectrums
in the hunger of a child,
suddenly green
in dusty sky
asleep in the eyelash
unites all curious things.

Rubén Darío's Voyage

On a fevered bed
reverie whispers
in Latin's obscure signs,
you wander the stars
suffering universal speech
full of poverty's dismissals,
absolute indifference to wounds
and a stranger's thin arms
spilling riddles
at nameless times,
seeking in language
revelations of solace,
sea voyages,
scattering Medusas,
unexplored globes,
Spanish proverbs
in red notebooks
watching Judas trees
empty their vineyards
of unjust solitude,
brambles of elegies
reunions deflowered,
on a night's chill
of unmasked griefs
unholy idols and tongues
scattering winds of words
plastered on city walls
for a revolution's
austere love.

Francis Ponge

Time shrivels
demolished fragments
of the sky,
crumbling a low wind
in a Paris garden.

Retrospective

Goya's politics
Blakean visions
orange Mondrians
Pollock's "Vision of One"
pink Degas dancers
betrayals in Gorky
Man Ray's cabin fever
Warhol spills
Picasso women
Whitman portraits
years of Apollinaire
Corot trees
concealed Rodin stones
hours of Watteau
tiny monochromes
Magritte reds
David Smith abstractions
Fouquet miniatures
hungry *cognoscenti*
liquid Matisse
Cézanne apples
Brâncuși sculptures
Jasper Johns aesthetic
escape into pop art.

Marilyn

Your mascara
has hidden us
the red, white, and blue
salesmen
who sell their nakedness
to Hollywood moguls.

Your blood
over the porcelain lies
of reporters,
the psychologists
the professors
the ballplayers
the producers
the dicks
who kill you.

I cut my wrist
and smeared my blood
on the stage of the drag show
when I saw your likeness.
Marilyn,
you belong to us, too.

O. V. de L. Milosz

With the dark river
a rose speaks
knowledge of the sky
on Jacob's Ladder
lifting a voice
to Abraham's bosom.

Umberto Saba

The winter is not distant.
You are expecting secrets
even in hiding
along the slim canal
of the empty harbor.
Your pasta is turning cold
listening to allied radio
with the echo of a poet
and the yellow star
pressed on your coat
by the white linen closet
until the tribulation
is over.

Keats

Keats, it is dawn.
You look up to the roof
taking refuge
in a strip of heaven,
believing the day sky
cannot deceive
the barren trees
of winter's randomness,
ice on the hilltop,
bread for sparrows
in a lost nest.
Nature tries to disguise
your deference
even to tasting death.
Your voice clears,
a magpie trembles,
you move papers,
drawing breath
from words.

Celan in 1950

Unaware of sunlight
your mind
swallows the steaming art
like uneven smoke.
You write with wisteria feelings
yourself a stranger,
you refuse black-forest cake
or to blow out candles.

Frank O'Hara in SoHo

Puzzled expression
with a four across
your open eye redder
than Warhol's "Soup Can"
slipping olives and dandelions
into a Greek salad
wishing for 4 a.m.
and daylight to unlock
a poor man's winter.
Outside icicles sob
past shuttered rooms,
you clench
a bit of Havana
and make a face
with prayerful ease
without even leavened bread
for a last supper.

Cendrars

Vague stars
from Paris to Hollywood
unsettled blind wishes
ripped vocal cords
a rumor's proverb,
your mirror
bites our faces.

Albert Marquet's Posters

Painting in morning
the right hand
lies flat over sunshine
unbuttoned in huge pockets
with the fiery tramplings
of whispers
at card tables.

The posters at Trouville
by the milk of constellation,
the barbs of bees
following exiled streets,
a couple of beggars
wish the ripest oranges
under the Zeppelin-sky wind.

And you by the riverrun
by unpacked boxes
third-class tourists
offering a deafened blue
under shutter shade,
your arms raise
on appraised canvas
carrying the cross-dressed horse.

Jacques Roubaud

Rain's indigo
by the harbor,
you turn
to prehistoric waters
wondering
if your carried memory
will bring
fragmented lava
to a poem.

Kokoschka

A vigilant exhibit
in the instant
of butterflies
subjected out of breath
gathering light
from pumice sky days
in the lasso of time
indurate with no sleep
mixing an arid death
out of terror
a bougainvillea
in the promised umbrella.

Marina Tsvetaeva

Bandaged nights
waiting for an augury
on abandoned landscapes
for a lover's cosmogony.

Jam Session

for John Cage, in memoriam

Sunday took up
soundproof rooms
of our genius.
I'm playing bass
of a ravenous jazz,
imploding fingers
in atonal clashes,
you on hurting piano
by a wind section
with improvisational
hands.

Drum rhythms
sound out in footnotes
by Big Apple taxis
of eerie urban noises.
We rehearse the cool
chromatic notes
of adolescent blues,
jumbling wanton distillations
and nerve-ending scales
carrying electric chords,
augmented beats,
frazzled metronomes strike
like a couple of pitchmen
moving in aesthetic time.

A Century Past

Closer to dialogues
on the sky's breathing
sunshine is angry
as the face
of Ida Kamińska
on the limitless lens
in daylight's mask,
every occupation
soiled by another Earth
scattering ink ashes
invisible on marshes,
mountain, sea, wall,
voices uncovered
prayers crucified
and every leaf tripled
on living branches,
fathering memory
of time's threshold
reabsorbed rain
devouring tongues
of disposed lines
in an actor's wounded
words.

Queneau

A monk's rise
to retrace
story by story,
a solo
that will be repeated.

Looking Away

for Larry Eigner, in memoriam

Like Borges or Milton
in a smaller universe
here in Boston
they look away
from your shadow
not recognizing in gesture
the blindness of disposition
seeing others pass by
only making time dying
more than clear-sky lovers
who forgot you resemble the living skill
trusting to your silence.

December Days

Half asleep
with a nonchalant air
you lean
on an open window
by insouciant curtains
ushering in noonday's sun.
Snow rides
on absurd rooftops,
bluejays move south,
ice blooms on chimneys,
while a poet hides
near a ring of fire,
a pure voice is driven indoors,
Callas sounds on the radio,
and time is hardly noticed.

Mondrian

Running by the loft
sunlight withers,
your panting disguises
then reinvents
an edgy maze
on blinded surface
with a bright wash
along Dutch parchment
reminding marred canvas
of dismantled visions
in your sleepless limbs
shaped by solitude
and traces of reveries.

Cioran's Wager

You expect
no one
or nothing
as you have
everything
in your mind
excepting
the wisdom
of the gods
who have no king,
but Caesar
is always at home.

Aragon

Incantations quiver
from red and blue veins,
robes stripped
from graves,
tales trickle
outside crematoria,
memory trails
at cemeteries,
they are not lost in you,
you knew them all,
defying bad times,
they still remind us,
barred windows
prisoner's screams
partisans on fire
labyrinths of exiles
refugees, unionists
resistance fighters
innocents who shook
before abstract torturers,
you cannot believe
but I believe you.

Edmond Jabès

Ages of bees
fly over schoolbooks,
a lost Talmudic time
in a tribe's memory.

"Out in the Open"

Today you belong
to a foreign body
wishing to escape
the public.
Even a private zoo
is no excuse
when locked like a beast.
City loudspeakers
are calling for peace,
no disagreement
yet the yellow breath
of a mangy summer
leapfrogs away.

You feel imposed upon
like memory's smoke dust.
If only you could be
a wild fawn.

At the Savoy

At the Savoy
the Armstrong sounds
while you in bloodless lips
bathe slightly warm champagne
asking me about "the Bird,"
your horse-shy face
shimmering in pink
with the hollow scent
of your former occupation,
citified from sleepy suburbs
and our right hard legs
move sideways to the flow
of the beat and beaten.

Brecht

Demanding praxis of air
among Berlin's rooming houses
dialectal language
plays on,
you search for a key
just for one night.

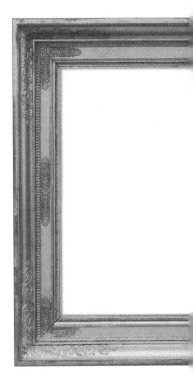

Flame

Reinaldo Arenas, in memoriam, 1943–1990

You were one of us,
where the sated night
could not hide your spirit
underground
with an ardor of justice
more radiant than any exile.

You breathed on the *auto-da-fé* flame
not fearing an unknown refugee
becoming a geomancer's shadow,
though you were in shark seas
locked up by powers
not greater than Poseidon's.

Let us light a candle
in your far-off absence
from all conflagrations.
I will not believe you are dead.

The Wharf

I couldn't admit
my lucky lot
at the open boat
returning to the wharf
to anchor in warm air.
Child in a sailor suit
mocks halos of his uncle
with Dalí's big beret.
Time stops moving
without a passport
on the backgammon table
near the blue-fringed map
the sea becomes earthy,
dust waves to us
from sheltering wind.

The child climbs
on laughing coral reefs,
gestures to the harbor graves
where night owls
throw love grenades.
The shore chimes
with bells in twelve tones
eying cuttlefish
in blue-black waters.
You find a year-old newspaper
and read it backward
with false death notices
and you, Hart Crane,
alive at last.

Larbaud

The eye of a bird
above carnival streets
of a caged Parisian.

Romantics

1. Schubert had it.

2. Stendhal felt it.

3. Nietzsche had nightmares of it.

4. Leo Tolstoy suspected it.

5. Balzac exposed it.

6. Proust feared it.

7. Gide hid it.

8. O. Wilde laughed at it.

9. Nations die from it.

10. A sore spot.

Ned Rorem

Your romantic notes
are wild
but tentative
ergo sum: (A E D G)
of part four
of your *roman à clef*.

Holding your visionary diary
in your coat of arms,
you hopscotch the universe
with every last resort,
cruise and cornerstone,
kicking in
each rendezvous' grief.

In your black robe
of morning's invincibility
or evening's burgundy
smoking jacket,
you find in your back pockets
your named and unnamed lovers.

Going down on every gesture
with an aboriginal sin,
you leapfrog
from each death
with no surrender
to your critical
and classical enemies
who invariably are a frieze
of friendless chamber players
knowing even the greatest
Gallic soloist
has his own lamentations
through scales not difficult,
no sleep can contain you,
no song.

Mishima

You left a skeleton
over abrupt lives,
uncovering a canvas,
poetic skulls
of nationalism,
tattoos, butterfly,
a man's bloody stone face.

Rimbaud

Finding out
how perishable verse
escaped all pallor
of speechless brainwashing
from parental storms,
you make mirrored gestures
to hide from a troubled noon
with a cyclone of words,
an excuse
to clear out anxiety
and diminish
the bullet's pure noise
from Q&A Russian roulette
in the mind's edginess.

Leaving imagination
and the joker
of a lost game
without injury,
wounds, memory
in the detention
of the exile
to create
a counterfeit correspondence
to insure a name,
myth, identity
for your lyrical prison songs.

Jacques Prévert

Your misfortune
ages in the rain
under an arsenal of clouds.
You imagine
a ride on swans
of the resistance.
You face
the children of paradise.

Klee

A snapshot over the sidewalk
blinds the climbing Luna moth
and the raw egg
of conscience
opens a voice in fatigues
from the window aisle,
breeds anemones
in lightbulbs for answers
and noose with art
elbowed by a crushed terror
totally interior.

Marcel Proust

Adrift in a century
invisibly drawn in,
you shudder on causeways
aching for art
calling for a pastiche
of rhythms
sentenced on sounds of maxims
by a sunny Chartres cathedral,
you close your veinal blinds
by rainfalls
a sentence never forgotten,
you map shells
brown strophes
with strokes
of skeptical pen
behind madness of characters
in a tubercular age.

Visiting Helen Vendler

You ask for a poem
even beat or unfinished
turning blue as my notebook
alone in the room
with a frozen smile
and naked strength
wishing to die there
after auditing Yeats
from the back of the class
indifferent to anything
but words.
"You have the gift,"
she whispers.

Bei Dao

On the hills
at dusk hour
flowers turn silver
by great waters.

Lorca at Seville

Gazing into shapes
of morning light,
your eyelids burn out
sands of words,
blinding like paperweight
on bluish pond.
A halo moves my hand
and your sunburnt arms.
The wind fades fast
by leafless dying trees,
even the air is silent
by six gulls in flight.
You sing arias
from Seville
expecting handwriting
any moment
from the sky,
unafraid of strangers
except for their armbands
along a hot dirt road
on the ormolu trail.

Edward Albee

Straights are too real
you said,
in the long hotel lobby
as the shoeshine boy
played footsie,
fell dumb
for two-toned happiness.

You mount the elevator
unwilling to sleep
with your eyes open,
sending up
for cold cuts
and German beer
with the gesture
of authority.

You, a stranger
to yourself
this night,
a new boy in town
a new play
in the backside
of your unofficial
duties to engineer.

Alain Veinstein

A rabbi exiled
in dark caves
whispers
the slaughter
of centuries.

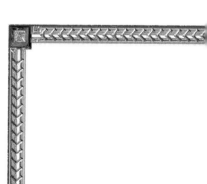

On Beacon Hill

for Robert Lowell, 1917–1977

We spent the day
after your lecture
an inclination to memory
footloose by verse
trying to be eclectic
ghosts facing and tracing
the sequence of your ancestors'
trees, clinging to olive branches
and the markings of your loving cup.

André Derain

Asking witnesses
of answers
extinguishes all notices,
the tenor of your times
unexpected afternoons
mad wines
cold coins
microscopic skin
terrorized Tarot
azured night
battered colors
doubt from organs
bandages appearing
from moving the wilderness.

Kierkegaard

You struggle
to hear the liturgy
in a cathedral of time.
Mozart burns
by the image
of the Virgin.
In your fatigue,
your unintended watch
speaks volumes
in your doxology.

Brâncuși

Inside the forearms
of half a century
eyes that slow voices
from toothpicks of wood
several faces stone
competing with explosions
of sunshade
radiant in the psychological
jaywalking as shadows
disembody keepers,
white goes outside
underlying handprints.

Jaccottet

Absolution, your wheat,
unforgiveness, your barley,
love, among the trees,
you hide in your pose.

James Joyce

Catching sleep
by the calls
of reckless birds,
you shelter
by the door
listening to echoes
from dead stones.

Kurosawa

On the screen
there are snowy undertakers
eternal gamblers
painful beggars
three on a road
without silk purses,
you hear a march
with a prayer drum.

Baudelaire's Lament

Days grow shorter
fearing silent organs,
you lapse from mimicry
into opaque past
without a future
except for Delacroix.
Insomnia won't erase you
nor will music's notes
sounding among signs
behind Persian blinds
on spring bed blankets
with undelivered kisses,
but it's only childhood
answering in the dark
until the first sun
of silence opens
to boundless air.

Stefan George

The sky asks its clouds
of sweat and dust,
what comets connect
or where do the shadows
of cicadas go
past linden trees.

Jun Takami

1907–1965

No one hears
the ocean's hardships.
You tie shoelaces
in a sunshine hunger.
The belied rice
drops from your hands.

Debussy Sonata

You stood at the piano
playing Debussy.
The sun tears
through jalousie windows,
your hair turning
as the light stills
toward the grandfather clock
and I, with empty rosin,
dreamed of that sonata
with the solace of cadenzas
quivering in bare iced sheets
for a private rehearsal
through pages of my wanton eye
always wishing
the velocities score
between time and space
to pronounce an affirmation
I practice the A, E, D, Gs
of a companion and friend
who will never leave me.

Borges' Last Day

Thinking of loss
in an open city
resting easy
on the hammock
breathing in astral justice
under shared sunshine,
dust blinded
by history's wrinkle,
a four-seasoned exile
needs the earth
to kiss
but cannot reach
for promises
under his blanket
and drinks in proverbs,
yet blue mountain waters
are distant as seashells
in a stranger's arms.

John Wieners

I watch you strut
over to the gymnasts
the muscle guys
who move along the Charles.

We never knew each other,
our flesh wants to camouflage us.
You are hurting, too,
but pride makes you
an unexpected god.

Music blares out
from a Spanish taxi.
You roll a beer can
along the street,
only a blind man
was listening.

A guy holds you up
near the doorway
hoping for justice or sex.

Jules Supervielle

Sorrow endures
concealing the night.
Incense wanders
through the sky.
A pigeon stays on earth.

Urban Reading

The exiled poet
without papers
passport
or green card
only with a letter
from Ginsberg
gets into the cab,
hears Coltrane riffs
and blues.
It starts to snow
on the windshield
tiny flakes
like stolen kisses.
The sky is absent
and the fare rises.
The hungry poet
jumps out the taxi
on asphalt streets,
hitches for a ride
on moonstruck miles.
A surrealist
with action paintings
in her car
picks up the poet
who goes to the university.
Ginsberg is there
with kisses for us.

Klee's Angel

Like moving
the wings
and cloudlets
of our history
the futurists
turn back to
acknowledge
the high art
embodied
in you.
"Angelus Novus"
speak to us
of possibilities
on an unshaven
earth timespan
where the voice
of fern and grass
belongs to us,
the ocean is clear
for salmon,
whale, and dolphin,
unpolluted city masks
now familial
be removed,
for wheat and grains
to again grow
on threshing floors.

Soupault

An orange cup full
of gliding wishes
becomes seeds
pulsing a sharp nostalgia
when your youth returns
from sea.

Proust and Vermeer

In precious enlightenment
from the sun at Delft
our mind rolls back
a canal of time
brighter than a memory
with a Dutch master
and French novelist
drinking from a Chinese tea glass
with fresh madeleine
met with yellow reflections
from the windows,
remembered of a still life
in lemony sprinkled moment.

Tell Me

Tell me on this Earth Day
I will get out
of my environment
to celebrate with Renoir
in nature's shifting winds
my own art of language,
that my memoir
of spending days
with him at the museum
and dreaming of his shaped
colors needs my innocence
to be in a metamorphosis
dream reconciled
but to get me away soon
from my wintry exile
into the butterfly sunshine
sitting by the window
watching the snowflakes,
hearing a bluebird whistle
at the slate roof shadow,
knowing spring will dawn
in neon light red
in sands of Earth Day
by thistle branches.

Jean Follain

On the fever chart
precessions
of goldenrod, gentian,
outside, the sunburnt waves
higher and higher
and it is hard to keep up.

Kafkaesque Images

Kafkaesque images so powerful
in the copper light
of a less-than-courteous sun
for an unguarded moment
commingling on us
by one red-eyelid photograph
staring at us
outdoors at a stop sign
at dusk watched by
spyglasses of unknown
cameras taking our pictures
by unauthorized visions
on parking lots
even after happy hours
beyond city limits
by auguries and juries
as backdrops of memory
haunting us while secretly
taking your prints.

Manhattan Riffs

Wherever a moon is sealed
here for my waiting gig
to play new sax riffs
the streetlights shine
on a leafless tree,
my friend sways
shading in
an oil portrait of us
or when fading out of love
watching a silent red sky
having lost hope
by the seaside green
yet composing a jazz solo
among rippling dunes
under a solitary gazebo
from my old telescope,
viewing the meteoric stars
above Brighton Beach
when Whitman or Crane
visited the Brooklyn Bridge,
those spans between
parental storms
of my own visibility
here in Manhattan,
writing in nine-circled bars
on this voiceless night
by an unmade bed,
anonymous sunglasses
a live elm
with my initials on it,
a comatose clock
with my name and memory
returning to me.

Hocquard

Myth and shadow
by a closed shop,
you knock in response
to pawn your life,
merely a guest
of the sun.

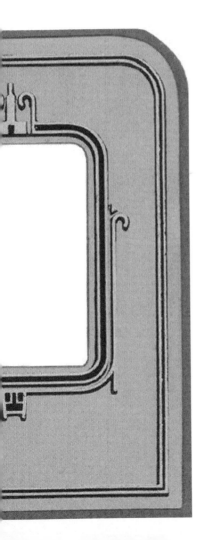

A Letter to James Merrill

1980

Dear J. M.,
my life is a peril.
Nothing but death and sex
can reach me.
I remember your petalled face
in your summer gear,
and you drinking ale by the pint.
Of course you ignored me
for Biarritz
trying to possess
what only God could guess,
those Cole Porter lyrics
or panegyrics
from your last poem.

You expected yourself
to be shot
somewhere in the dark room
with the big shots
of Yale or Hollywood.
I told you
simply, James,
"Be good
be understood
praxis not practice
rhyme when you reason,"
but you would not believe me.
You preferred
the *raison d'être*
of the inaccessible.

On Cambridge Common

for Elizabeth Bishop, 1911–1979

My shadow
in yours
as it yields
to awareness
of your long spell
at day's end,
here by evergreen
a thousand years old,
by a deafening guitar
on parched grass,
sharing with students
a timeless memory
when you returned
dazzled from Brazil
with new bubbling images
flinched by camouflaged cold
in white-kerchiefed dawn
by snow gardens
on Cambridge Common
with nothing but song
between us.

Dali's "Enigma"

That desire
of beguiled lament
in the tinted
white-haired dye
of decomposition
clutching the fish head
in the red-spotted
upper body
of paralyzed
countenance
of daggers
between the murmur
of still life
and fetid death
by lady's slipper
implanted by
your foreground
plans of memory
in automatic chicanery
of ironic persuasion
joined with the space
in the grotto
by deep central figures
of speechless suffering
paralyzed by mother
and son
contorted by space
and the grasshopper
holding a knife of time.

Weil

A saint whitewashed
in troubled handcuffs,
an ache of loving wounds
on grindstones.

Joy Street

Memory so close
to earth
through the eyes
of hundred-year
evergreens
up on the hill
of poets,
Plath, Lowell,
Sexton,
all passed,
eclipsed by legends
and the open-air fervor
of nameless heat
over narrow attic voices
from red-brick buildings
uncovering the hatless
of maddening psyche
over academic
and streetwise sounds
of mouthpiece traffic
dodging the void
in each seasonal circle,
and landscapes
change in Boston
along the Charles River's
unforgotten tone.

Picasso's "Corrida"

Turning its heavy
yellow and red
green and blackened
blends,
Pablo with
a vast canvas
for the wounded
horse intertwined
with contours
of the wrestled
heaving-shaped bull
sagging with paint
where Orphic beauty
of bleeding innocence
resolves to clear out
agony's painted
evil character
of anthropomorphic war
and the wide-eyed focus
of emerging political
arenas
in antagonistic form.

Paul Claudel

Ambassador on oceans
where signatures hide
a nightmare of faith.

The Print

You kept
the little Fauve
print you found
at a yard sale,
checked it had no
monetary value,
wondering if it were
lost or stolen
during the war,
yet its fire orange
kept you
in wild-palm joy,
knowing
all art
like words
are alembic alphabets
and colors
splashed on canvas.

A New World

Those wild strawberries
in our cool hands
keep us in sweetness
on long, airy days
we hike Concord trails,
ablaze the meadow flowers
in well-worn denims
through kicking a ball
by cypress,
catching my breath
over tall grass shade
against west wind,
swarming hum of bees
by Walden Pond,
reading to a circle of students
overcoming the pinecones
on common ground
over Indian blankets
of spreading light,
all of us in turn
reciting Thoreau,
responding with perception
among relentless sunshine
on these dales and hills
as nature reveals
the same language, love, nature
that the songbirds call.

Camille Claudel

Your bronzed hands
turned on Rodin
in a parlor of mirrors,
a noble genius
scoffed on a daybed death
with stones in shambles.

Going Underground

In memory of Robert Lowell, 1917–1977

In a tweed jacket
when Boston scatters
morning
a chill descends
on your walk in the rain,
forgetting your umbrella
along the Esplanade,
a lone acid face passes,
his "Good day"
covering his own pain,
trying to think Emerson
or James is still alive.
At least to reach the station
is to die known
and go underground again,
to remember a poster
at the old corner store
from unseen departures
when fictions carry us over,
embraced by time zones
on alphabet street signs
of cool interruptions,
wishing to lie back in bed
or be a year younger
when signs, visions, rumors
open early
by grandfather clocks
on common speech,
as words crack
open water drops
of lethal insomnia

decoded in your absence
almost supremely human
with rotting laughter inside.
A button falls off your suit
pushing your way out
of jammed train stations
to cross the lowest level
in belief's suspension.

Soutine's Painting

I could not get away
from the green
in Soutine's visibly
attainable
"Man Walking the Stairs"
that silent morning
when my eyes rested
on the museum's
desk catalogue
with a calm shade
at nature's own shivering,
leaving me breathless,
tuning my alto sax
here by village houses
on a fingerless vacation
for only a day,
blunted by breezes,
wave their disappearances
under most high hills
from branches extended
to trusted grasslands
in miles of sleeping music
sweeping boundaries
now immortal.

Hugo Claus

In a Holland
in colder times
a solitary poet
blocks the madness
of those evicted
from the earth.

Recognition

Gunnar Ekelöf, in memoriam

Her memory
in permafrost
riding boots
on nameless roads
of a zigzag life
on undated winter
latitudes
awaiting consummate
sunshine
in absent skies.

Louis Aragon

A letter from a worker
before the war,
roses will outlast
even the elixirs
of justice and politics.

All These Earthly Things

for Juan Gelman, 1930–2014

All these earthly things,
the small myrtle at the edge
of the pond's tall grass
as Mexican fruit falls,
sponging Juan's sandaled feet
near the pomegranates,
a nomad poet in solitude
on his hammock
senses an allergic hay fever
near an Argentine raspberry stalk
where an exile
from the Ukraine
by the hunched valley
locates carpenter bees
by woodland sounds,
while students search for turtles
taking photos of their carapaces
for nature classes
by scales and nets of fishermen
in a sky wall of early blue gauze
over the hospital ship docking
with its odor of cold milk
with rain on the horizon
by open barnyard fields
of slender curled tendrils
where the poet collects shells
to hear echoes
for his blank notepaper
near the ocean grove
watching
the hauling of lobsters

in undulant waves
with many gulls crying
at noonday
as this moment in time
is suddenly baptized
in fizzled raindrops
as tiny birds with hidden wings
curled on branches
sing of Juan Gelman
in the eventide searching
for his missing daughter
by a harpoon found
from ditch waters.

Summer Blues

A Beat poet
cooped up like a parakeet
in a New England winter,
tired of TV screens
reruns of faded old films
clouding over
his bloodshot eyes,
wanting to be a runaway
or a Rimbaud
here in Vermont
with a red French wine,
French croissant,
takes out his sax
to play riffs
along the Green Mountains
yet afraid to be
terrorized from a waterbed
abandoned from home
and his made-up exercise
on the trampoline,
to take up alto clarinet.
A lost friend from the band
shows jazz's balancing act
in his disturbed universe,
as my kid brother
throws a football against
a city graffiti wall
found from the Patriots
locker room,
telling him a Chinese proverb,
"Tension is who you think
you should be, relaxation
is who you are."

Warhol's Factory

Eclectic chair
silk screens
mirrors upon sheets
falling boxes
blood-stained ellipses
black blocks
mixed imitations
on mimeographed lattice
circular stone
shrapnel metallic shaped
autographs
stamped out, "do it"
color fields
monochromatic
red grid,
an eccentric glance
with time.

Pierre Jean Jouve

Your words gave birth
on a chilled twilight.
Around you the underground
speaks in whispers.

Sartre's Tongue

In corners
that *Seventh Seal*
our action paintings
nix motives
in expressionist contours,
your legacy
in our dry mouths,

with exiled alembic
words even when
our body politic
digs into aloneness
losing ourselves
without recording
answers to history
connecting the whole
world systematically
in art's dialectic

of ultimate fashion
we choose a finality
of negative denials
except for art's
bourgeois politeness
turning away
from fetish fascism
church or state
drawing the defaced
and abject objects
to intervals of a matrix
of geometric sculpture
in linear lines
of our intuition
in poem and freedom.

Tanguy's "Dark Garden"

Branch loss of
limbs by faceless
bleed of unnatural
expressions
looming murals
in patterns
and striped
overrunning
the oeuvre
of matchless trees
bizarre-shaped
watercolors adrift
in formless pools
of still life
sinking at ponderous
shades of forest
in pitch
of shadowy firehouse
wavy ashes
at the rock-filled
abyss.

James Schuyler

I do not know
why you were obsessed
with last year's
flowers and boys
at Fire Island
last year's Hockney
last week's poems
or Garland's last song.

Perhaps you were sentimental
or just nuts
ignoring the newspapers
and the parrot
you got for Christmas,
out on the foul town
with two on your arm
halfway between romanticism
and the realism
of the street smart,
you who knew it all
believed it all
saw it all
dreamed it all
and now outlast us all.

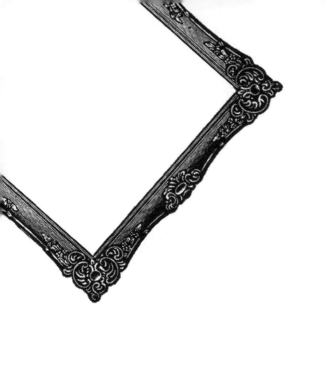

About the Author

B. Z. Niditch

was born in 1943, a war-child violin prodigy who came of age in the era of Beat and Post-Beat poets, and claims Marcel Proust as his favorite author. He is a poet, playwright, fiction writer, teacher, and aphorist, as well as the founder and artistic director of The Original Theatre in Boston, which has presented original, experimental plays on contemporary social and political themes since 1990. His work has been widely published in journals and magazines throughout the world for decades, including *Columbia: A Journal of Literature and Art*, *The Literary Review*, *Denver Quarterly*, *Hawaii Review*, *Le Guépard* (France), *Kadmos* (France), *Jejune* (Czech Republic), *Leopold Bloom* (Hungary), *Antioch Review*, and *Prairie Schooner*, among other outlets. He lives in Brookline, Massachusetts, and has published numerous chapbooks with small presses, including *Captive Cities*, *Lorca at Seville*, *Fugitive Poet*, *Terezin*, *Boston Fall*, *Childhood*, *Freedom Trail*, and *Everything, Everywhere*, as well as a collection of his aphorisms, *Dictionary of the 21st Century*.

Colophon

The edition you are holding is the First Edition of this publication. A few of the micropoems first appeared in a discontinued short chapbook edition, also called *Portraits*, published by Alternating Current Press in 2008, and a few poems first appeared in a discontinued chapbook, *The Poet*, published by Alternating Current Press in 2002. This expanded edition has never before been published in its entirety.

The title font is Rosabelia, created by Solid Type. The subtitle font is Futura. The Alternating Current Press logo is Portmanteau, created by JLH Fonts. All other text is Athelas, created by José Scaglione and Veronika Burian. All fonts are used with permission; all rights reserved.

The Alternating Current lightbulb logo was created by Leah Angstman, ©2013, 2019 Alternating Current. The Wardenclyffe Series logo was created by Leah Angstman, ©2019 Alternating Current. The frame graphics are in the public domain.

Front cover artwork: "Ghosts 157." Artwork by Ashley Parker Owens. Property of Ashley Parker Owens, ©2019. Used with permission; all rights reserved. Ashley Parker Owens is a writer, poet, and artist living in Richmond, Kentucky. She has an MFA in Creative Writing from Eastern Kentucky University and an MFA in Visual Arts from Rutgers University. Find her on Facebook at facebook.com/ashleyparkerowens, and find her résumé at ashleyparkerowens.wordpress.com.

All other material was created, designed, edited, or modified by Leah Angstman. All material is used with permission; all rights reserved.

Other Works from
Alternating Current Press

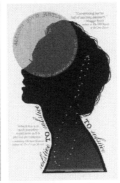

All of these books (and more) are available at Alternating Current's website: press.alternatingcurrentarts.com.

alternatingcurrentarts.com

Made in the USA
Middletown, DE
15 May 2019